Wish and Win

Win

The Sound of W

By Alice K. Flanagan

2

This is a wish.

This is a wink.

6

This is a wig.

This is a wag.

10

This is a well.

This is a wall.

13

14

This is a wick.

This is a walk.

18

This is wind.

This is a win.

Word List:

wag	wig
walk	win
wall	wind
well	wink
wick	wish

Note to Parents and Educators

The books in this series are based on current research, which supports the idea that our brains are pattern-detectors rather than rules-appliers. This means children learn to read easier when they are taught the familiar spelling patterns found in English. As children encounter more complex words, they have greater success in figuring out these words by using the spelling patterns.

Throughout the series, the texts provide the reader with the opportunity to practice and apply knowledge of the sounds in natural language. The books introduce sounds using familiar onsets and *rimes*, or spelling patterns, for reinforcement.

For example, the word *cat* might be used to present the short "a" sound, with the letter *c* being the onset and "_at" being the rime. This approach provides practice and reinforcement of the short "a" sound, as there are many familiar words made with the "_at" rime.

The stories and accompanying photographs in this series are based on time-honored concepts in children's literature: well-written, engaging texts and colorful, high-quality photographs combine to produce books that children want to read again and again.

Dr. Peg Ballard
Minnesota State University, Mankato

The Child's World®
childsworld.com

Published by The Child's World®
1980 Lookout Drive • Mankato, MN 56003-1705
800-599-READ • www.childsworld.com

ACKNOWLEDGMENTS
The Child's World®: Mary Swensen, Publishing Director
The Design Lab: Design
Michael Miller: Editing

PHOTO CREDITS
© allou/Shutterstock: 18; Annette Shaff/Shutterstock.com:
9; Blend Images/Shutterstock.com: 21; Denis Kuvaev/
Shutterstock.com: cover; Elena Zajchikova/Shutterstock.
com: 13; Emmoth/Shutterstock.com: 14; Julia Kuznetsova/
Shutterstock.com: 6; Julie DeGuia/Shutterstock.com:
5; NataSnow/Shutterstock.com: 9; oceanwhisper/
Shutterstock.com: 10; Sergey Novikov/Shutterstock.com: 17

ISBN 9781503809246
LCCN 2015958475

Printed in the United States of America
Mankato, MN
June, 2016
PA02310

ABOUT THE AUTHOR

Alice K. Flanagan lives with her husband in Chicago, Illinois, and writes books for children and teachers. Ever since she was a young girl, Ms. Flanagan has enjoyed writing. Today, she has more than 70 books published on a wide variety of topics. Some of the books she has written include biographies of U.S. presidents and first ladies; biographies of people working in our neighborhoods; phonics books for beginning readers; informational books about birds; and career education in the classroom.